No Smoking, No Drinking, No Drugs

Sally Huss

Copyright @2016 Sally Huss
Huss Publishing
All Rights Reserved

ISBN: 10: 1-945742283
ISBN 13: 9781945742286

It was a day like any other winter day, as Billy walked home from school.

But when he rounded a corner, the day changed. There on the steps near an old building was a group of older kids who were all laughing and joking. They were also smoking and drinking.

"Here, kid," said one, "take a puff."

Another offered him a drink, shoving a glass in his direction.

Just as Billy was about to take a sip, a little mouse jumped out from behind a bush.

He held up his hand and waggled his finger at Billy. "No. No," he said. "Tell him 'NO'!"

The little mouse was so insistent; Billy did what he was told. "No thank you," he said and handed back the glass.

Then the little mouse waved for Billy to follow him.

Down the street, the little mouse hopped up on a wall and introduced himself, "I'm Mr. Consequences. I'm here to help you make good choices."

"Con… con… con… " Billy stuttered.

"CON-SE-QUEN-CES!" said the little mouse. "It is what happens when you make a choice. Smoking cigarettes, drinking alcohol, taking drugs, and vaping are all bad choices. Bad choices lead to bad results. Let me explain."

Mr. Consequences pointed to a row of houses across the street. All had smoke curling out of their chimneys. "Smoking is for chimneys," he said. "Not for people, young or old."

He continued, "Chimneys are made of bricks or stones and the smoke that passes through them does not harm them.

But the walls of your lungs and throat are made of living cells and smoke can harm them over a period of time."

Jumping down from the wall, he added, "Just as smoking can damage your throat and lungs, alcohol can damage other organs of your body…

… like your heart, liver, kidneys, and even your brain."

They walked a few steps together, but Mr. Consequences didn't want Billy to miss the point, "You need these organs to function well to keep you healthy and happy."

With that, the little mouse pulled out a piece of cheese from his pocket. "Look in here," he said. "This is what can happen to these people."

He held the cheese up so that Billy could peer into it.

What he saw was a group of people who all looked sick and unhappy. "When you lose your health," said Mr. Consequences, "you lose your happiness too."

"What about drugs and the people who use those?" Billy asked.

"Drugs are for doctors," explained Mr. Consequences. "Sometimes drugs are needed to help a person who is sick or injured get well. But, a doctor is the one to decide this.

The drugs that kids use on the street are damaging to your health too, especially to your brain. You need your brain to function perfectly so that you can become the best you can be.

Everyone has the ability to become great at something, or even many things. Drugs can get in the way of this, and a person, young or old, may lose interest in learning and developing their own greatness."

Again, Mr. Consequences held up the cheese for Billy. "This is what can happen if those kids continue to take drugs," he said.

There, through a hole in the cheese, Billy saw a bunch of young people all lounging around on a street, doing nothing. They looked lazy and hopeless; they were no longer happy.

"Oh, no," said Billy sadly. "Then why do they do it? Why do kids smoke and drink alcohol and take drugs?"

"Many like to do what everyone else is doing. Most don't know the consequences when they start. It's very simple, if you don't start, you won't have a problem. If you do, you might."

The little mouse handed him the cheese. "I'm glad that now **you** know the consequences, Billy," he said. "That's what is important. **Your** future is bright. Take a look."

There in a hole in the cheese, Billy could see his future. He was pleased by what he saw.

"Well, I must be off now, Billy," said Mr. Consequences, as he hopped back up on the wall. "Remember, everyone has the right to make their own choices – good or bad.

I believe you now understand the importance of making good choices. Your happiness depends on it."

"Thank you," Billy replied and waved goodbye.

Mr. Consequences called back, "You're welcome, Billy. Don't forget, good choices lead to good results; bad choices lead to bad results."

Billy was happy now that he knew the difference and planned to stay healthy and happy his whole life long.

The end, but not the end of making good choices.

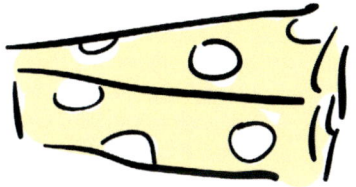

At the end of this book you will find a Certificate of Merit that may be issued to any child who has fulfilled the requirements stated in the Certificate. This fine Certificate will easily fit into a 5"x7" frame, and happily suit any girl or boy who receives it!

Sally writes new books all the time. If you would like to be alerted when one of her new books becomes available or when one of her e-books is offered FREE on Amazon, sign up on Sally's website – sallyhuss.com.

If you liked *No Smoking, No Drinking, No Drugs,* please be kind enough to post a short review for it on Amazon. Thank you.

Here are a few Sally Huss books you might enjoy. They may be found on Amazon along with the rest of her extensive collection of books designed to delight and inspire!

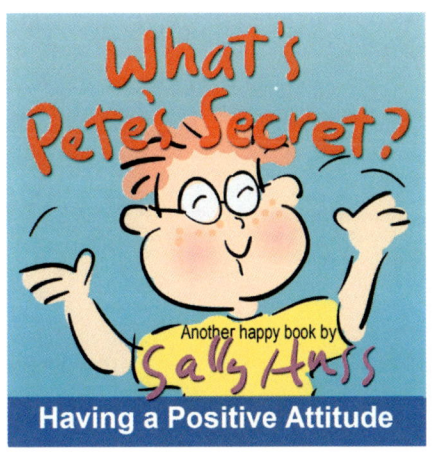

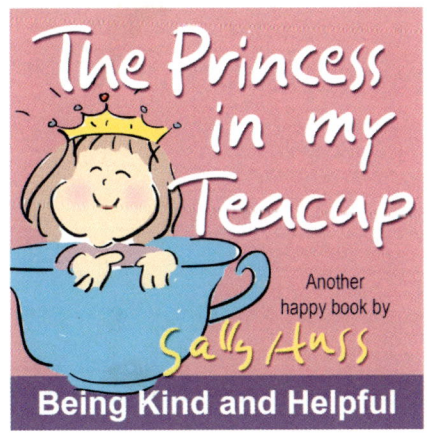

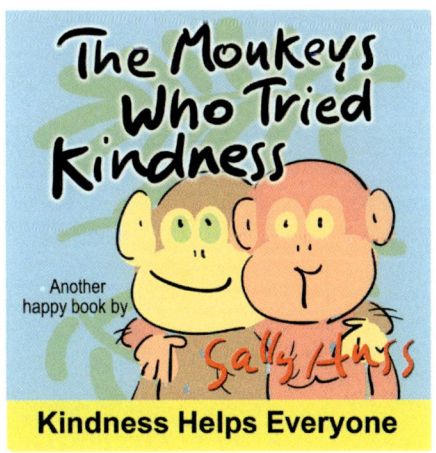

About the Author/Illustrator

"Bright and happy," "light and whimsical" have been the catch phrases attached to the writings and art of Sally Huss for over 30 years. Sweet images dance across all of Sally's creations, whether in the form of children's books, paintings, wallpaper, ceramics, baby bibs, purses, clothing, or her King Features syndicated newspaper panel "Happy Musings."

Sally creates children's books to uplift the lives of children and hopes you will join her in this effort by helping spread her happy books.

Sally is a graduate of USC with a degree in Fine Art and through the years has had 26 of her own licensed art galleries throughout the world.

This certificate may be cut out, framed, and presented to any child who has earned it.

Made in the USA
Middletown, DE
17 July 2020